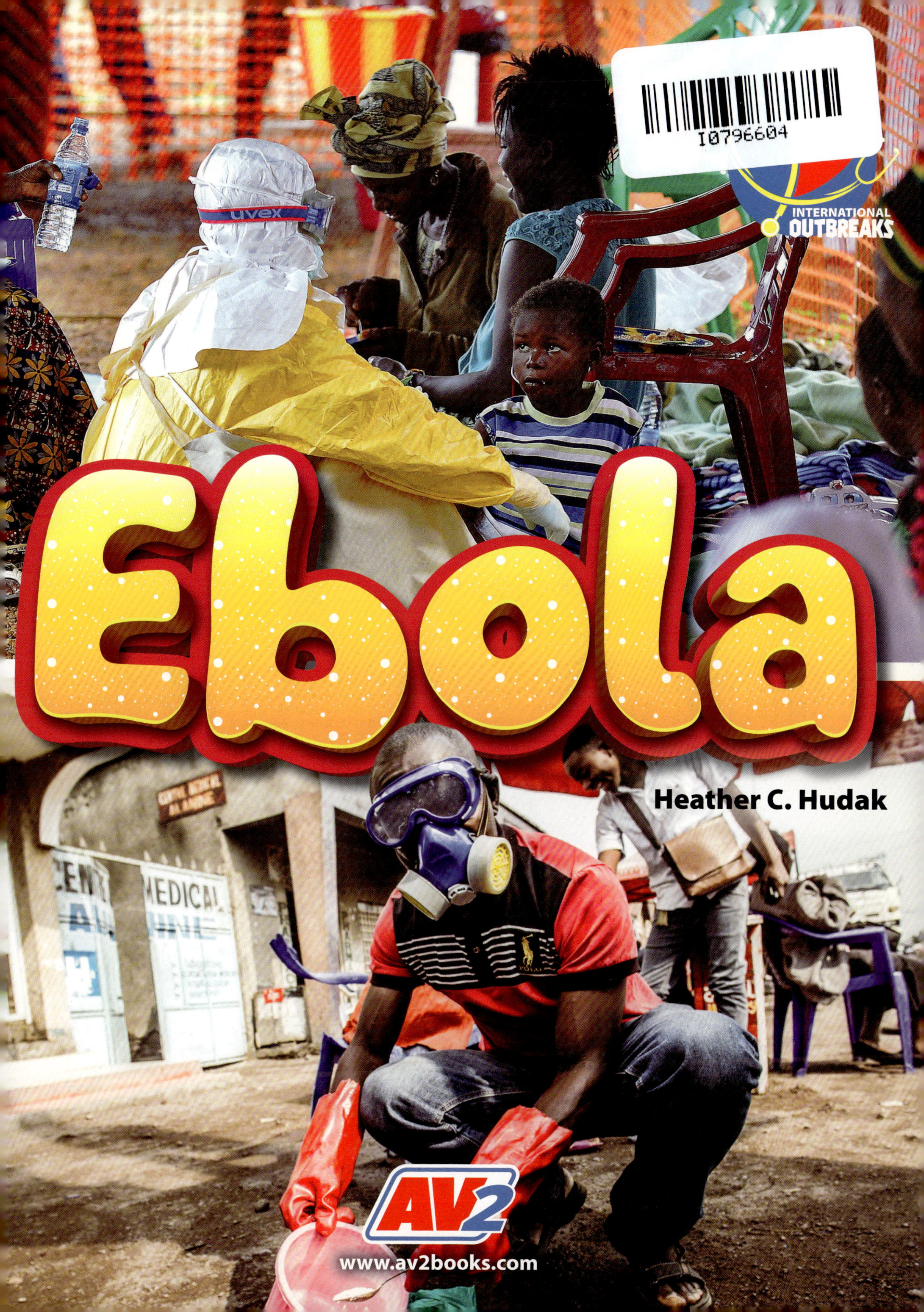

Ebola

Heather C. Hudak

AV2
www.av2books.com

Step 1
Go to **www.av2books.com**

Step 2
Enter this unique code
ZGPDWYVZH

Step 3
Explore your interactive eBook!

AV2 is optimized for use on any device

Your interactive eBook comes with...

Contents
Browse a live contents page to easily navigate through resources

Audio
Listen to sections of the book read aloud

Videos
Watch informative video clips

Weblinks
Gain additional information for research

Try This!
Complete activities and hands-on experiments

Key Words
Study vocabulary, and complete a matching word activity

Quizzes
Test your knowledge

Slideshows
View images and captions

... and much, much more!

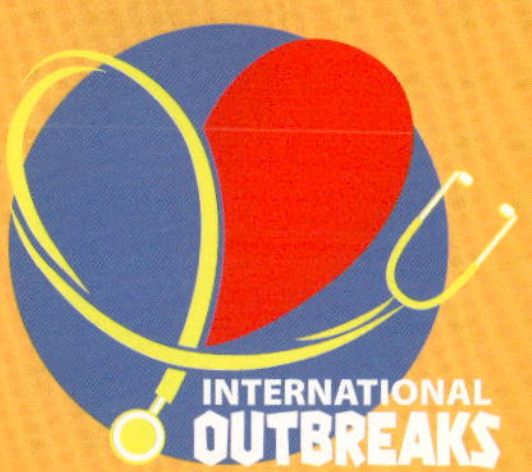

Ebola

CONTENTS

Wearing special suits, masks, and glasses can prevent healthcare specialists from catching infectious diseases.

Breaking Out

There are many kinds of **diseases**. Scientists track how often they occur and where they take place. This helps them know how many people normally get the disease in a certain time and place. An outbreak happens when a disease **infects** many people in a short time. There are more cases of the disease than expected.

An epidemic is an outbreak that occurs on a larger scale. It happens when a disease is not well **contained**. This leads to a sudden increase in the number of people infected in an area. The disease then spreads to other areas. It may even reach different countries. This happened in 2014 when the Ebola **virus** spread through West Africa.

FAST FACT

The World Health Organization (WHO) is part of the **United Nations** (UN). It is responsible for the health and well-being of people all over the world. WHO decides if a disease is an outbreak or an epidemic.

Health experts need to work in the field to stop diseases from spreading.

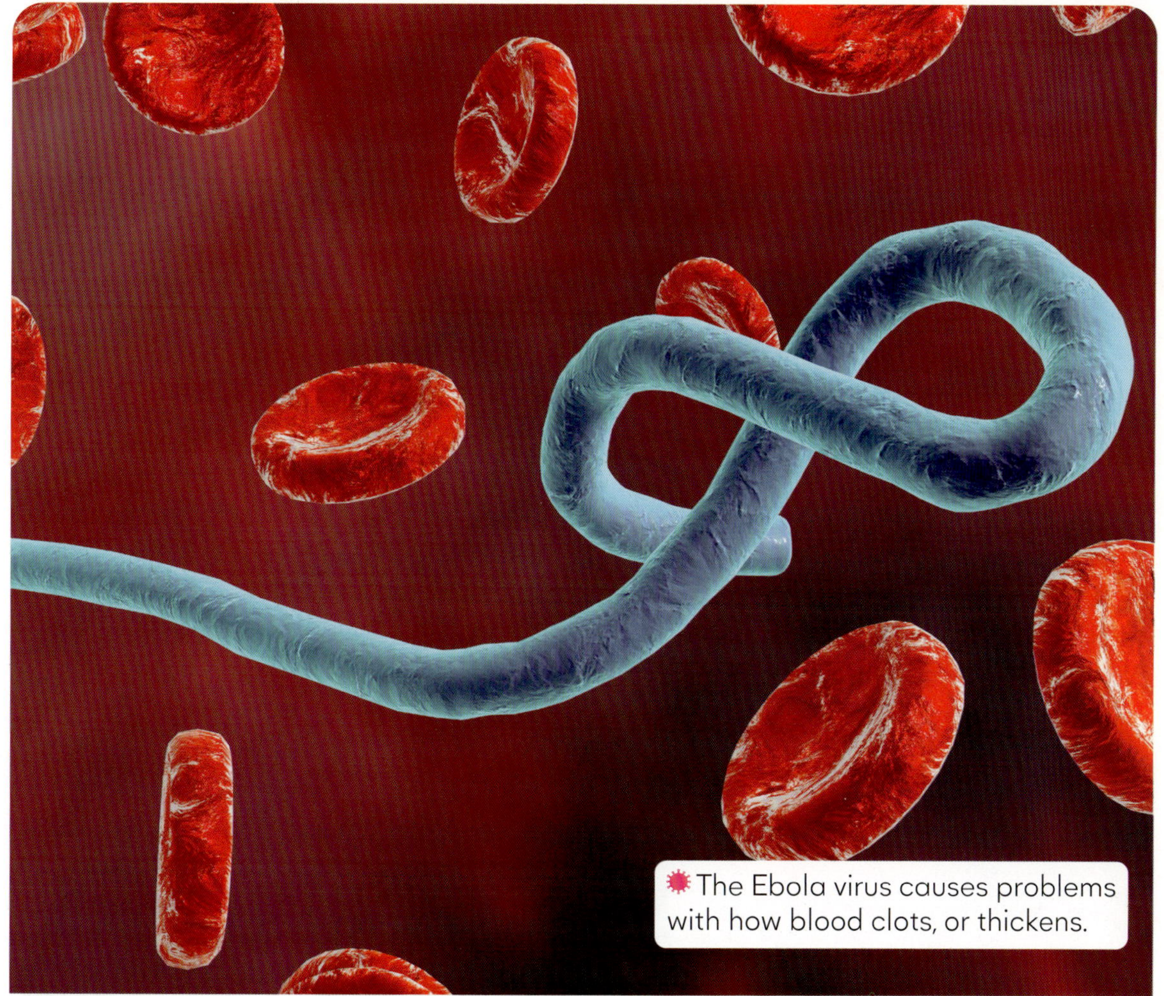

The Ebola virus causes problems with how blood clots, or thickens.

What Is Ebola?

The Ebola virus existed long before it spread to humans. Ebola affects humans and other primates, such as monkeys and gorillas. People who get the virus can die. Ebola is very rare. It is only found in a few parts of the world. Most Ebola outbreaks take place in Africa.

Ebola was first discovered in Central Africa in 1976. There was an outbreak in the Democratic Republic of Congo (DRC). The disease was named after the nearby Ebola River. A second outbreak took place in South Sudan around the same time.

Regular handwashing can help destroy viruses.

Spreading the Virus

Ebola is **contagious**. It can spread from person to person. Doctors think it can also spread from infected wild animals to people. Bats, porcupines, forest antelopes, monkeys, and gorillas are some of the animals that may carry the Ebola virus.

To get infected with Ebola, a person must touch the bodily fluids of someone who has the virus. Blood and tears are examples of bodily fluids. The virus can also be spread by touching objects that were in contact with infected bodily fluids. These include needles, bedding, and clothes.

Viruses can only be seen through special microscopes.

Staying Safe

Ebola only spreads through bodily fluids. It does not spread through the air or water. People who live with an infected person are most at risk. Health workers must wear personal protective equipment (PPE) to avoid getting Ebola.

Signs, Symptoms, and Treatment

People start to show signs of infection 2 to 21 days after they come into contact with the Ebola virus. Most people get a fever or feel tired, at first. Over time, the symptoms may become worse. An infected person may start to have stomach pain. Some people bleed for no reason. Red eyes, skin rash, and hiccups are also signs of Ebola.

There is no known cure for Ebola. Drugs can be used to help infected people feel better. Some drugs are used to lower a fever. Others prevent infection. Some people may get oxygen to help them breathe. Those who survive Ebola have **antibodies** in their system. Antibodies can protect people from getting Ebola again for up to 10 years.

Many viruses, including the Ebola virus, cause fevers. Officials may check people's temperatures to help keep the spread of a virus under control.

Symptoms of Ebola

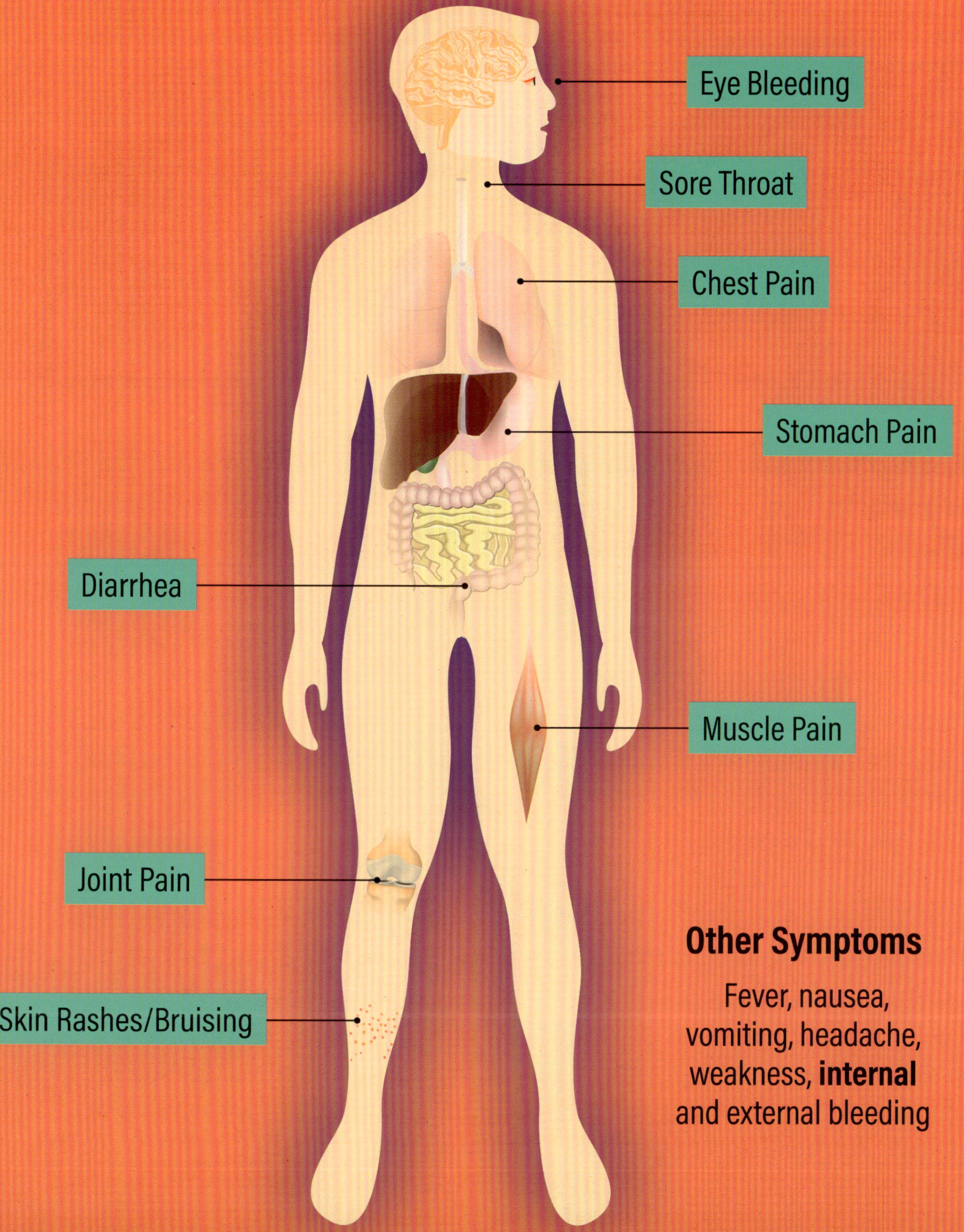

Other Symptoms

Fever, nausea, vomiting, headache, weakness, **internal** and external bleeding

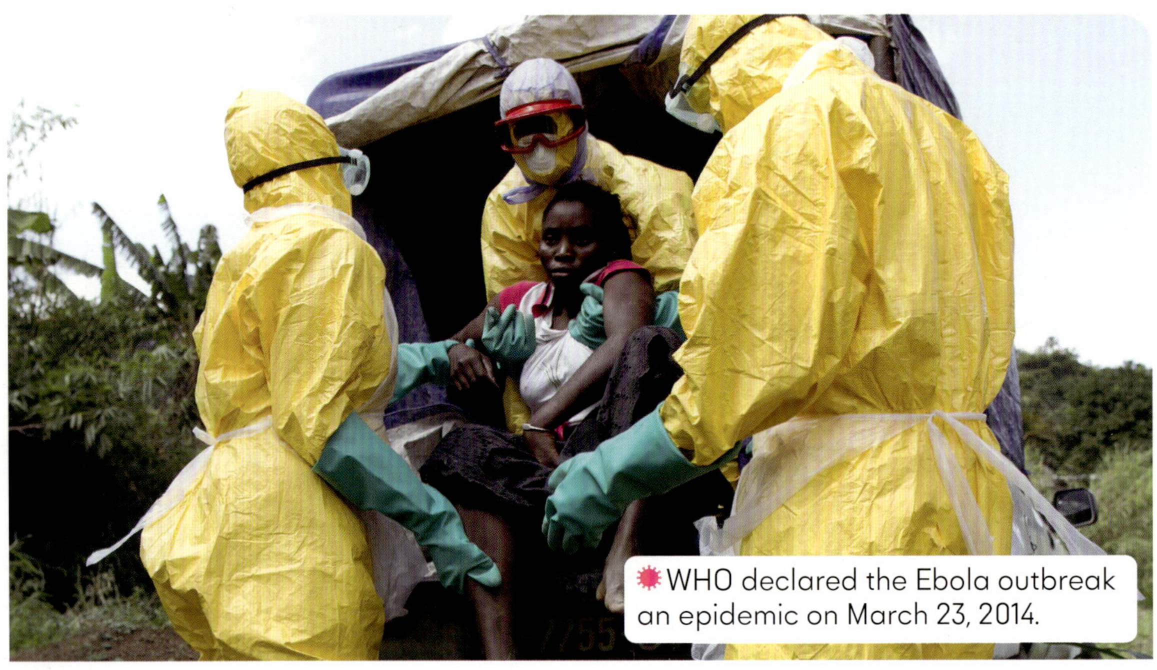
WHO declared the Ebola outbreak an epidemic on March 23, 2014.

Ebola Outbreak, 2014 to 2016

The largest Ebola outbreak in history began in West Africa in 2014. It lasted until 2016. More than 28,600 people were infected by the virus. About 11,300 died. Doctors think the first case was a baby in Guinea who may have caught the virus from bats. His family fell ill next. The health workers who treated the baby also became sick. So did others who came in contact with the infected people.

There was poor public healthcare in the area. Many people lived in crowded spaces. This helped the virus spread to other countries. Ebola quickly made its way to Sierra Leone and Liberia. By June 2014, the virus was out of control. Leaders of the infected countries worked together. They put policies in place to stop the spread. WHO helped. The spread of the virus began to slow down. By June 2016, the outbreak was over.

Mapping the Ebola Outbreak in Africa from 2014 to 2015

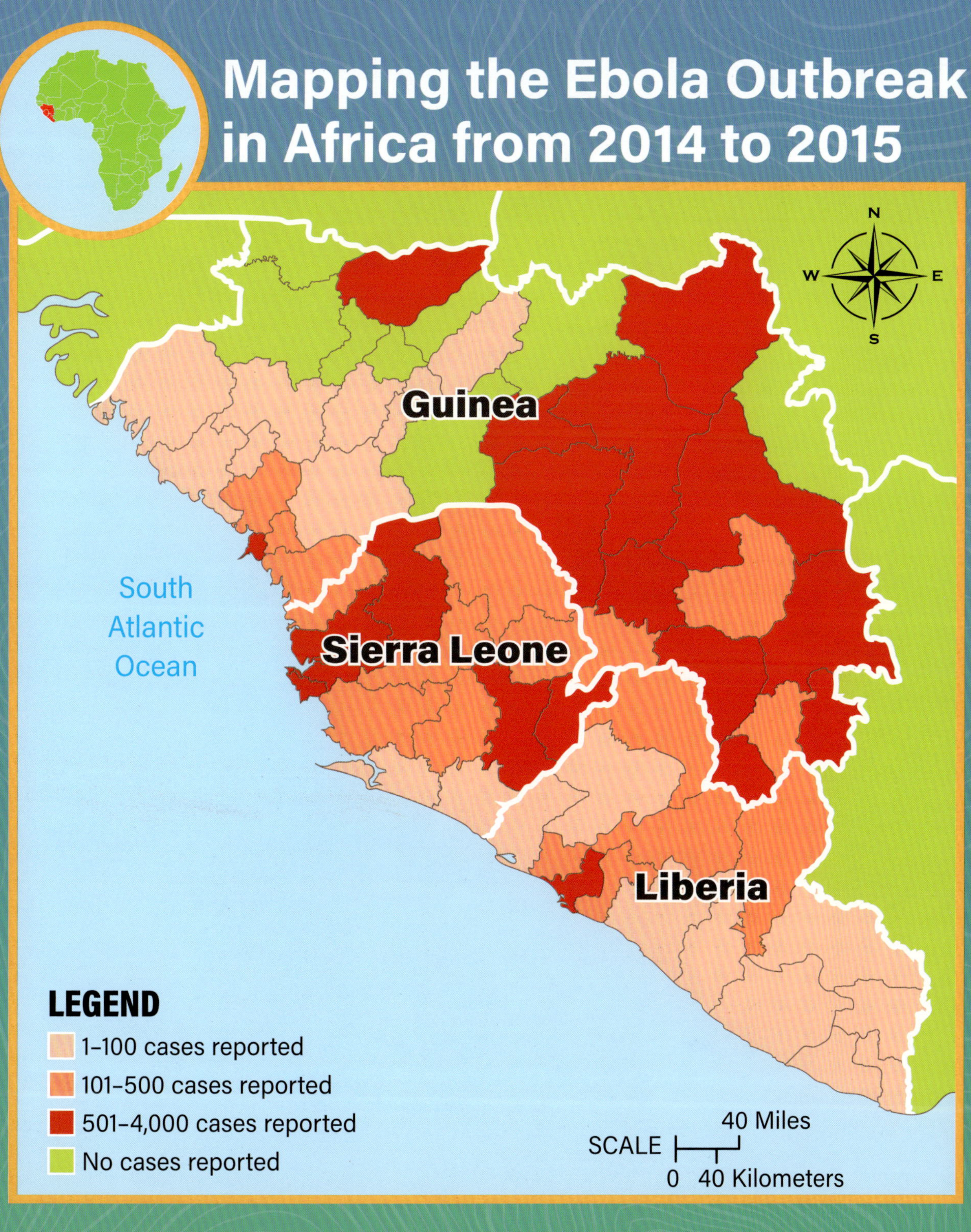

Countries close to Guinea, Liberia, and Sierra Leone were at a higher risk of experiencing Ebola outbreaks during the epidemic.

Global View

Countries around the world sent help to Africa in 2014. The United States sent hospital gear and gave millions of dollars to the cause. Cuba sent a medical team of 165 people to help in Sierra Leone. The United Kingdom, Canada, France, and many other countries also helped out.

Travel **restrictions** were put in place in several countries, such as Australia and Canada. People coming from West Africa had to be tested before coming into the United States and the United Kingdom. Many governments warned citizens to avoid traveling to West Africa. Only a few cases spread outside of Africa. Most of those were health workers or volunteers who had been in Africa. These people were quickly treated to prevent the Ebola virus from spreading to their own countries.

Perspectives

Most people thought that travel restrictions were the only way to stop the spread of the Ebola virus. Other people thought that these measures were too extreme. What do you think?

SPORTS FINAL

DAILY NEWS

NEW YORK'S HOMETOWN NEWSPAP

EBOLA SCARE IN CITY

PAGES 4-5

- Man tested for deadly virus at Mt. Sinai
- Disease 'unlikely' but docs 'don't know'
- Test result looms as NYers wait in fear

Science and Research

Scientists came up with an Ebola vaccine in 2015. A study was done on thousands of people in Guinea. Half of the people were given the vaccine. They did not show any signs of Ebola 10 days after being vaccinated. However, 23 people who did not get the vaccine caught Ebola in the same time frame. This gave scientists hope that the vaccine would work on more people. They did more testing. The vaccine was approved for widespread use in December 2019.

The best way to stop Ebola is to prevent it. People should avoid contact with wild animals that may carry Ebola. It is also important to avoid contact with anyone who might have Ebola. People who care for Ebola victims need to wear gloves and other special gear. They should wash their hands often and avoid touching objects that could be infected.

FAST FACT

Ebola is very deadly. Between 25 and 90 percent of people who catch Ebola die. Almost 50 percent of the people who were infected in the 2014–2016 outbreak died.

Vaccines are substances that can help prevent the spread of diseases.

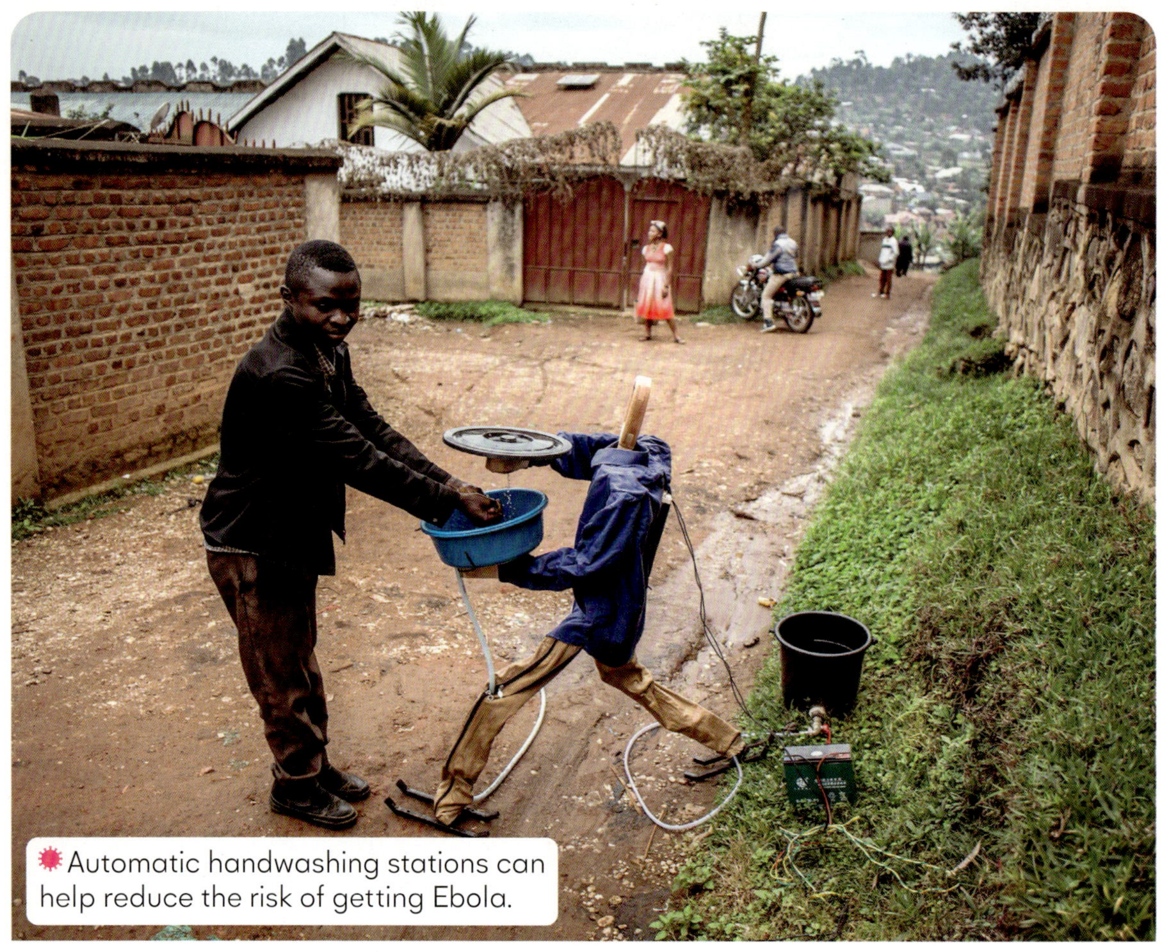

Automatic handwashing stations can help reduce the risk of getting Ebola.

Ebola Today

Ebola is still active today. The second-largest Ebola outbreak in history hit the DRC in August 2018. It was the largest outbreak that the country had ever seen. By 2020, the number of new cases was going down. The outbreak was under control.

Ebola outbreaks make the news all over the world. There are pictures and stories of sick people in need of help. Many stories are shared on social media. This is why some people fear Ebola will come to their country. They think they will get very sick. Not all of the information that people read is true. It is important to get facts from trusted sources. Ebola is only a **threat** in a few places. The chance of it spreading to others is unlikely.

Ebola Cases in the Democratic Republic of Congo by July 2020

Ebola Timeline

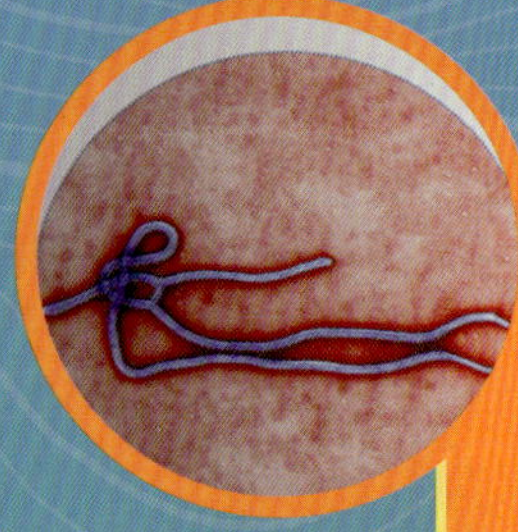

1976
Ebola is discovered in the DRC and South Sudan.

1995
Ebola strikes the DRC, causing 315 cases and more than 250 deaths.

2000
Uganda has 425 Ebola cases and 224 deaths.

2001–2006
Small Ebola outbreaks happen across Africa.

2007
Ebola breaks out in Uganda. There are 208 cases and 78 deaths.

2014–2016
The largest Ebola outbreak in history takes place in West Africa.

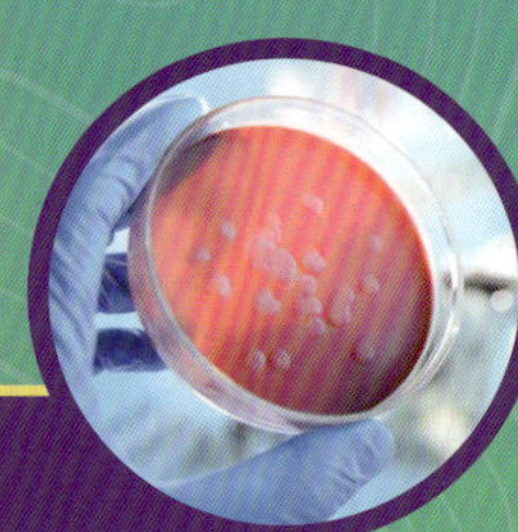

2018–2020
Ebola hits the DRC in 2018. By 2020, more than 3,000 cases are reported.

ACTIVITY
Spread the Word

A great way to stop the spread of a virus is to tell people about it. Posters are put up in public places across Africa. They show people how they can stop Ebola from spreading. Try making a disease awareness poster of your own.

1. Brainstorm ideas. Then, choose a topic. Proper handwashing is one idea you could use.
2. Come up with three questions about your topic. For instance, you might want to know what you should use to wash your hands. Then, research the answers.
3. Use pictures, words, and graphics to make a poster. Think about how you will make it interesting for people to look at. Be sure to explain why the information is important.
4. Put your poster up for others to see.

EBOLA QUIZ

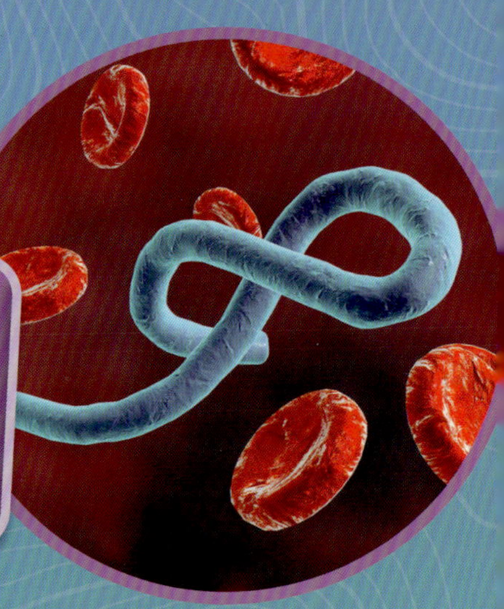

1
When was Ebola discovered?

2
Is Ebola contagious?

3
Where was the first Ebola outbreak?

4
How does Ebola spread?

5
Who can get Ebola?

6
How can people stop the spread of Ebola?

7
When was the largest Ebola outbreak in history?

8
How is Ebola treated?

ANSWERS

1. 1976
2. Yes
3. The DRC and South Sudan
4. Contact with the bodily fluids of an infected person
5. Humans and other primates
6. By avoiding contact with people or objects infected with Ebola, regularly washing their hands, and wearing proper gear
7. 2014 to 2016
8. With drugs and oxygen for the symptoms

Key Words

antibodies: substances that are made in special cells of the body to help fight off infection
contagious: moves easily from one person to another
contained: kept under control
diseases: illnesses that have certain signs and symptoms
infects: contaminates a person or object with a disease-causing germ
internal: inner parts of the body
restrictions: limits on what a person can do
threat: something that is likely to cause damage or harm
United Nations: an organization that maintains peace and cooperation among countries of the world
virus: a very small germ that gets inside the body and spreads

Index

Get the best of both worlds.

AV2 bridges the gap between print and digital.

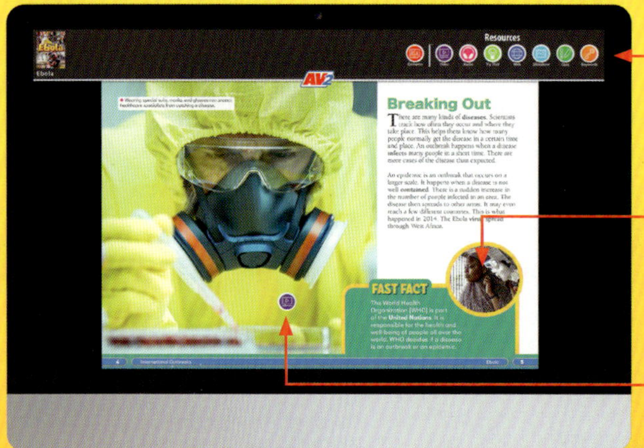

The expandable resources toolbar enables quick access to content including **videos**, **audio**, **activities**, **weblinks**, **slideshows**, **quizzes**, and **key words**.

Animated videos make static images come alive.

Resource icons on each page help readers to further **explore key concepts**.

Published by AV2
14 Penn Plaza, 9th Floor
New York, NY 10122
Website: www.av2books.com

Library of Congress Control Number: 2020943889

ISBN 978-1-7911-3222-4 (hardcover)
ISBN 978-1-7911-3224-8 (softcover)
ISBN 978-1-7911-3223-1 (multi-user eBook)
ISBN 978-1-7911-3225-5 (single-user eBook)

Printed in Guangzhou, China
1 2 3 4 5 6 7 8 9 0 24 23 22 21 20

082020
101119

Art Director: Terry Paulhus Project Coordinator: Priyanka Das

The publisher acknowledges Getty Images and Shutterstock as its primary image suppliers for this title.